Love Notes to Grievers

Love Notes to Grievers

tending to grief after loss

Angela E. Morris

POWNAL STREET PRESS
CHARLOTTETOWN

www.pownalstreetpress.com

Pownal Street Press is an independent press that broadens the publishing landscape with a diverse collection of non fiction and children's picture books.

Love Notes to Grievers • ISBN 9781778124587

Printed in Canada by Friesens. Edited by Mo Duffy Cobb & Danielle Loewen. Author photograph by Lori Glaseman. Designed by Jordan Beaulieu. The text was set in Adobe Garamond.

Our books may be purchased for promotional, educational, or business use. Please contact your local bookseller or Pownal Street Press at hello@pownalstreetpress.com to purchase.

Pownal Street Press gratefully acknowledges Mi'kma'ki, the ancestral and unceded territory of the Mi'kmaq First Nation on whose land our office is located.

For dad, you didn't have many words for your grief.
Because of you, I do.

CONTENTS

AUTHOR'S NOTE

Writing about grief and death was not where I thought my life would go, but do we ever set out to write about the complexities of grief before we get harpooned by it?

When I started sharing my writing online, people began sending me messages about how their grief felt validated by my words. With that in mind, this book's goal was to share further what the body, mind, and relationships go through in early grief based on some of my experiences. The dominant culture* in North America diverts us from our grief. The impact on our well-being is enormous.

It is a culture that sighs in relief when someone's grief is digestible, not too much is shared or seen, and not too little to observe so they know you aren't a monster—just the right amount so that the people around you aren't in too much discomfort. Death brings up fear. Grieving displays what most people try to avoid, the thought of someone they love dying.

Words are never adequate when describing the experience of heartbreak from the death of a loved one, or from someone you had a complicated relationship with. Still, some of us try with tender accuracy to be a soft landing for each other, seeking comfort through writings on grief and loss. If you're reading this, chances are you're grieving or you know and care about someone who is, and you are trying to understand their pain to support them. It's excruciating to accept that life has forever changed—living in the fog of your former life, especially in the beginning.

I share extended reflections on the following pages, shorter notes interspersed throughout, and some personal essays. For those who are already enlightened versions of yourself, my book may not be for you. My grief was initially quite messy, so throughout the book, I share essays highlighting that. There was nothing self-actualized about how my grief unfolded the first year after my dad died, but I am reasonably proud of where I am now.

You won't find any spiritual bypassing fluff here, if that's what you are after. There is no toxic positivity either. This book is for people who are in the depths of grief, who have lost relationships while grieving, who are feeling slightly feral, who are a bit ragey, who are a little lost, who are confused, or those seeking words of comfort, maybe even clarity.

I hope these reflections make you feel your grief is seen, and that the love for those who have died—or whatever kind of loss you are carrying—is reflected in these pages.

I know what it's like to be unable to concentrate. Please take your time with this book.

---

*Dominant culture

1. *Established norms, values and preferences as the standard for an entire group of people.*
2. *In a society the group whose members are in the majority or who wield more power than other groups. (Sparknotes.com)*

INTRODUCTION

Life changes fast. Life changes in the instant. You sit down to dinner and life as you know it ends. The question is self-pity. Those were the first words Joan Didion wrote after her husband, John Gregory Dunne, died of a heart attack in their New York City apartment at 71. She writes about it in her memoir, *The Year of Magical Thinking*.

It was the first grief-related book I listened to. Late at night, curled up in a ball on my childhood bed just days after my dad took his last breaths. Unable to sleep. Feeling lost, I took in Didion's words. I found myself in her experience, different yet the same. I didn't read it because I couldn't. Later, I would learn that a temporary cognitive impairment might happen as you grieve. It took me years to pick up a book and read more than a few sentences.

My dad was diagnosed with terminal cancer two days after I attended my friend's funeral. A tragic loss that I was deeply grieving alongside her loved ones. All in shock and agony over taking her life at 34.

I left my life behind on Vancouver Island where my partner and I had moved only three months before. I cared for dad as did my mom and brother for the four months of his illness back east. A year later, during the peak of the COVID-19 pandemic, my beloved grandmother died too.

I started writing about grief and loss after my dad's funeral. I wrote quite a bit before that, but it was all I wanted to write about after. I would jot down how grief felt in my body. On my phone in the notes app I wrote about my disorienting experience of the outside world as I grieved, comparing it to my world which had dwindled to the size of my dad's bedside. Our family home became a secluded island.

I wrote about how I felt about having empty grief platitudes lobbed my way too many times to count. *"I wish I could bring your dad back for you,"* a distant friend texted. I wrote about the crushing feeling I had in my chest that wouldn't leave. I wrote about friends and acquaintances acting in odd ways. Soon after, I registered for Megan Devine's course, Writing Your Grief, which was thirty straight days of writing. I opened my email each day to a new writing prompt. I wrapped myself in a blanket on the couch, wore the fleece robe that I had lived in while caring for my dad and continued wearing it daily for the first year after his death. Finally, I donated it. A tear-soaked souvenir I was dying to let go of yet oddly attached. I hugged my laptop close to my stomach, legs up, perched like a bird on the couch. An awkward angle to write, but I didn't care. I wrote relentlessly each day. There, I attempted to make sense of the pain in lieu of drowning in it. Sometimes it was both. Tears ran down my cheeks, and anger surfaced. My grief demanded to be known. I continued writing almost daily about grief for the next three years and counting.

In my early grief days, most days, I wanted to live in a cave with Netflix and copious amounts of chips and never come out. This motivated me to share more of my grief writing publicly to help others feel less alone, including myself.

When I returned home a few weeks after the funeral, I went back to work as a Massage Therapist. I struggled with my breathing as I got un-settled back into my life. My lungs felt like they were in a vice: constricted and bogged down. These symptoms were another aspect of grief that shocked me—the physical expression of it.

The heaviness in my chest and shortness of breath would build like a dam and then burst, resulting in a dramatic collapse on the couch, where I would stay for hours, exhausted. I cycled this way for months.

I kept forgetting to eat. I had no appetite or desire to prepare food. I would sit in the shower from exhaustion and let the water fall onto my face, chest then back, rotating like a rotisserie chicken to soothe my aching back and neck muscles.

I suffered from headaches, which eventually morphed into migraines. I feared that I may be having a heart attack leading me to get two ECGs, but it was due to being underweight at the time. The prolonged stress crushed my sorry excuse for a nervous system.

My safe place was the couch, where I spent many hours feeling frozen in time, joking to my partner that the floor was lava.

He later named it *"Couch Island."* The Isle of Couch is just off the coast of Bitter Anguish, around the bay from Another Friend Doesn't Understand My Grief and south of That Friendship Bites The Dust. Have you heard of it?

Begrudgingly, I put on work clothes. Having to wear pants instead of my robe and participate in standard hygiene practices only inflamed my exhaustion.

I was a wounded animal bleeding from its limb, but no one noticed because I wrapped the wound so well.

How grief affects you mentally, emotionally, and spirituality shows up in your body. It demands to be tended to, not fixed. I stumbled through the traumatic aspects of my experience, which expressed itself with physical symptoms and a short fuse in the beginning. The heaviness lifted when I gave my grief the attention it deserved. I was opposing the dominant culture's influence of moving on quickly, burying it, or keeping it palatable for others.

Most studies focus on the psychological aspects of grief and less on how it impacts the body. That is starting to change with the research and work of Dr. Francis O'Connor, author of *The Grieving Brain*, and her new book, *The Grieving Body*.

There is pressure on people to perform society's "acceptable" bereavement norms instead of honouring the uniqueness of each person's experience and lovingly supporting them through it. Alongside that, the sanitization of death and the loss of grief rituals and practices lead to a fragmented society. One that upholds hyperindividualism and encourages us to avoid or condemn our valid emotional responses, diminishing people's suffering and numbing emotional responses when going through a difficult time.

Your grief asks for the opposite of what dominant culture demands: speed up, disconnect, consume more, numb out, be productive, act strong, buck up, find the silver lining. Show everyone how together you are and get on with it. These cultural norms encourage you to bypass emotions. We stuff them down until we break down or burn out.

Grief turns your life upside down, shakes you to the core and infuses your insides with insurmountable pain while life rips on at a speed that feels relentless, even cruel at times. We may be living our grief differently, but some of us find each other because of it.

My way was to write through it, in it and around it. I became acquainted with society's ways of *managing* broken hearts vs *holding* them. There were several moments when my dwindling capacity to cope with the outside world brewed on my insides. I refused to stuff down my pain. I declined to perform being "ok" for others, even if it sent me down a few too many shame spirals as I grieved. I rarely betray myself for someone else's comfort but had to take responsibility for the moments when my hypersensitive reactions took over. I eventually had to go on an apology tour and get myself into therapy to help me cope with the overwhelm.

Wherever you are—be it early grief, somewhere in the middle, or decades beyond—your grief matters. The profound losses you're carrying do too.

No one is exempt from grief, although it comes with all the nuance and variety of experiences that our lives and relationships do.

We all become grievers at some point. It's only a matter of how and when it changes the trajectory of our lives that differs.

LOVE NOTES 1

name what hurts

No one gets to tell
you how to heal.

Grief, for me, has been the ultimate undoing—a complete rebuild—a pile of rubble to sort through.

The arrival of insurmountable pain has connected me to the world's aches more vividly.

Grief has broken me down and woven me with humans who dance between two worlds, one before their loved one's death and one after.

In grief, people don't heal by being made to feel broken and beyond repair. You are not broken. Your heart is.

People heal when you allow them to tell their stories, make space for their sorrow, and process what happened—the love so bravely shared with someone no longer here. That doesn't make you broken or weak; that makes you human, and being a human is hard.

It’s ok to name what hurts.

It’s ok to name what hurts.

It’s ok to name what hurts.

It’s ok to name what hurts.

It wasn't until people I deeply loved died that I fully understood the tending I am doing.

I finally grasp why no one can fix this. It's not something to fix but to awaken.

It's the spectrum of grief that allows the light, the beauty, and the broken to mingle together.

We must tend consistently and diligently to these layers.

Please remember that even mental health professionals misunderstand people's grief because the grief model some follow is not for the living: "denial, anger, bargaining, depression, acceptance."

That model is suited for a person dying of a terminal illness, not for people who are continuing to live with grief from the death of their loved one.

Not all therapists are trained in grief therapy.

Find one that validates your process and holds the proper space for you to go at your own pace.

I know how hard it is to see outside your grief in the early days.

Your brain is in a fog, and your heart is so shattered that you can barely breathe.

You will be brought to your knees, and you will get back up.

Be patient with yourself.

In grief, I ask myself what I need.

A hug—
Someone to listen—
A shower—
Silence—
Deep breaths—
To lay on the floor—
A walk—
Food—
A nap—
Water—
To cry—
To write—
To move—
To be in nature—
To wear my person's clothes.

What do you need?

Trying to make space for your grief in a society
that makes you feel broken and too
much for loving your people so profoundly is
why we have so many souls screaming on
their insides.

Tend to your grief.

Honour your love.

It's easy for people to assume that you're asking too much of them, but maybe all you are asking for is a little grace.

Grief

needs

GRACE.

No one is having the same
experience in grief.

Do not waste energy comparing
what isn't yours to live.

Grief is the ache and
the medicine for the ache.

Grief from a parent's death

feels like you want to go home

but can't ever again.

THE FREEZER SECTION

I cried in the grocery store, gazing into the freezer at the ice cream. My dad and I ate it for dinner. We ate it for lunch. It was all he could stomach close to his death. Together we sat on his hospital bed in the dining room, our white ribbed ramekin bowls loaded to the brim.

One of those ice cream days ended with me bursting into tears, landing my head on his lap, no longer able to hold it in. "I am just so sad, I am so so sad." I could barely get the words out. He patted my head as I snuggled in closer, him also in tears, which had become a regular occurrence since he received his terminal diagnosis. I had never seen him cry as much as he did in those last months of his life. His tears were a beautiful gift and an opening for healing. My upbringing lacked emotional awareness, a household that didn't speak to grief lingering in the air. A sea of suppressed emotions. Silences fell over our house. At times, low energy at Christmas, drinks to numb the pain, and unexplainable bad moods that would confuse my mom and me. My dad got lost in another time and place, at random, reminding us he was the only surviving member of his family. A sensitive man unable to express how he struggled with these losses. Buried deep but never gone away.

We slowly came to terms with what was to come, a brutal reality of loving him so profoundly. Reluctantly I watched him fade away, too quickly to process. And him poetically going through the five stages of grief, yelling "fuck" from his wheelchair in his anger phase. His sunken eyes and cheekbones, his legs now the size of mine, a gut-wrenching remembrance while sitting on the shower floor every day before heading downstairs to face reality. His death would bring grief no matter how beautiful the ending. No one could have prepared me for the death of a parent gone too soon. 65.

In the early days and months after, memories flooded my body everywhere I looked, reminders of Dad and my friend T, the most vibrant light gone too soon, her tragic loss ever-present. A pretty long blonde-haired look-alike with a wide-brim hat made me a gloriously sad water foundation of tears in public.

Surrounded by living memorials, I developed a keen awareness that separated the trivial from what mattered most but, in the early days, brought so much pain in remembering—my year of firsts.

Over and over, I said to myself, *My dad is dead*, my mind ruminating over it. The ice cream was dad's ice cream, the song on the radio was dad's song, and the GMC truck driving by looked like dad's truck.

Telling people, *"My dad is dead,"* did not carry the weight I thought it would. Sorry for your loss. Those words became empty. The bare minimum. Everyone continued with their lives. *"My friend took her life."* People winced. Sudden and stigmatized. *"My grandmother died during the Covid-19 pandemic."* We said our last goodbye over the phone, which stirred up too much sorrow for one body to hold.

From diagnosis to death, his rapid decline, her tragic ending, my sweet grandmother's last days met with restricted access to her. I felt hollowed out—a walking, talking human, though I wasn't sure how I was doing it.

These ordinary moments and reminders:

wide brimmed hats
a beard, with glasses
a song on the radio
a dad and daughter, holding hands
his favorite ice cream flavour
the smell of vicks vapor rub transporting me to my grandmother's side

Made me weep.

LOVE NOTES 2

emptiness / ceremony

Seek ways to ritualize your love and grief and tend to your pain. Be gentle with yourself and your body—slow, soft, and patient.

Savour and hold onto a few of your loved

one's clothes, rings, hats or whatever else.

You can create rituals around these items.

Ritualize your grief.

Do what feels good to you.

Death isn't a singular event where you continue as usual once the funeral and "recommended" mourning period ends.

A before and after is now formed. A tidal wave of emotion. Homesickness lodged in your stomach. A dream they are there, then gone when waking. Making peace with stardust you cannot touch, feel the ache long after the "sorry for your loss."

Share stories of your grief so that when other people enter this realm, there will be a soft place for them to land with less guilt for refusing to mask their pain for others' comfort.

When grieving,

we learn

what “ritual”

truly means.

Everything

becomes

ceremonial.

Breath becomes sacred because breathing
becomes hard.

Tears become a hymn.

The smell of their shirt, holy.

The retrieval of self before grief, never again.

In grief, we learn to create daily rituals for
who we have lost, what we have lost.

Forever carrying forward our loved ones who
are no longer with us.

Everything we do feels connected to this.

That is grief.

That is love.

That is the ceremony.

You live with insurmountable grief
until it loosens its grip on your chest.

You live with vivid memories of loss while feeling pressured to make your grief more palatable for others and doing that can feel too big to hold.

Find ways to help your chest soften
and expand.

Find people who allow your chest
to expand and soften.

Until you have experienced grief from the death of a loved one, you have no idea of the mental exhaustion that happens and how sensitive you become to the insensitive actions of others.

Expressing anger and sadness is frowned upon because it is too messy, and people like tidy emotions. Grieving the death of a loved one is excavating your old self. You are standing in a new life, and not everyone will know how to be with you in it.

PROPANE MAN

Shortly after my dad died, I yelled at the man filling the propane tanks at my parents' house. He was grumbling about how the snow wasn't shovelled, so he could get to the tanks easier. The snow removal saga had been going on for over a month. The company was leaving messages about not servicing our house because the drivers complained that there wasn't a clear path to the tanks. No one in my family had the energy to call back. Not one of us could stand to say, *"we are too exhausted to get to that because my dad/husband is actively dying in the VERY house you won't service in the middle of frigid winter, causing my dad stress right before his death, so kindly FUCK OFF."* No one wanted to explain why we had become the "inconsiderate snow people" on Waukegan Road.

Inside, we administered morphine, topped up IV fluids, assisted bathroom trips, washed dad's hair in the kitchen sink, picked up supplies for the nurses, learned to change out ostomy bags, and spent our last days together between trips to the hospital and one frantic trip to the emergency room after trying one dose of chemotherapy. He was already too weak for the recommended palliative treatment. Somewhere in the middle of this, we forgot to shovel the snow.

When one of the propane workers returned two days after dad died, the house was quiet. My mom and I were wrapped in blankets on the couch watching HGTV home renovation shows, a sanctified ritual for grief—

watching mindless shows that typically don't talk about death unless a widow is moving to Mexico on *House Hunters International.*

I looked out the window to see him kicking the snow, muttering to himself, and preparing to leave. I whipped open the door and cried, "Sorry! My dad was a little busy *DYING* to get to that!" and slammed the door full of rage. I opened the door again and, mixed in with a lot of swear words and tears, said, "You have NO idea what people are going through in these houses, so show a little respect." He stared, eyes wide. If he did respond, I don't recall what he said. Nothing was going to bring my dad back, so I wasn't interested anyway. I felt like John McEnroe, the legendary American tennis player known for his intensity and aggressive demeanour, yelling at the chair umpire but the *dead dad edition.*

This indelible outburst sticks out in my mind, how my grief-stricken emotions were hard to control at that time. It was inconceivable that people were living their lives unchanged while mine fell apart.

I lived in two worlds. In one world, people naively live without the heartbreaking reminder of who is missing from it. *Their people are still alive.* The other is where I struggled to learn to carry my grief while living with a gaping hole in it, conceding that grief and joy eventually find a way to come back together. It does but never the same.

No one could return my old life to me, the one with my dad in it. The propane man, angry about a bit of snow in his boots, was oblivious to that snapshot of heartbreak he was witnessing. My dad would never have snow in his boots again.

LOVE NOTES 3

it's not you, it's them

Your pain is not the problem. The problem is an impatient society demanding that you pretend you are already ok when you are not.

Healing takes time. Grief is forever.

That is what causes the most pain to grieving hearts.

Grief doesn't need urgent fixing—it is a slow burn back to yourself, a healing path like no other.

Honour yourself.

Honour your love.

You do not need to hand over evidence to prove you are worthy of the grief you are feeling after the death of a loved one. A relationship that depends on your performance entices you to reason instead of feel—to give away your power for approval, accept the unwritten conditions placed on the relationship, and act in ways that appease others and betray yourself.

You cannot heal around those who try to bury you.

The clearer you become

about what hurts,

the less you betray yourself.

PROLONGED GRIEF

Prolonged grief has been added as a disorder to the DSM-5—the *Diagnostic and Statistical Manual of Mental Disorders.* Feeling shamed, unsupported, and pathologized for grieving in a specific way for longer than a year has become a topic of conversation in the medical and grief literacy field. Grief advocates like myself believe that dominant cultures respond to grief in unhelpful ways and the lack of collective competency prolongs suffering. Because of that, many feel the pressure to hide their grief from others.

The lack of understanding, nuclear family isolation, useless grief platitudes, late-stage capitalism, alienation from social groups after loss, and ignorant advice on how to get "over" grief often add to that suffering. Trauma, oppressed identities, geographic location, socioeconomics and mental health also play a significant role.

I sit somewhere in the middle, the idealist who knows there would be less trauma and mental health struggles alongside grief if we lived in a healthier, less grief-phobic society. Where people have the support to grow their capacity for their grief and have their basic needs cared for, and without having to transform their grief or rise from the ashes or make the death of their loved one into a hero's journey. This reality would create less pressure to bypass the pain, act strong, or feel the need to prove you are worthy of connection when you are struggling—making it easier to metabolize your grief in a less stressful environment. A privilege that many don't have.

I have learned to make my grief a home. To tend kindly to it while also acknowledging that people suffering trauma alongside their grief may need extra support, which could mean getting a formal diagnosis for prolonged grief, or trauma, or both.

Grief is a response to loss. Grief is as natural as breathing, and is simply the practice of learning to live without someone you love. Grieving doesn't fit into a capitalistic system, which demands that you continue to be productive despite what you are going through, with little respite or relief.

You cannot bootstrap heartbreak. We should be pathologizing the systems in place, not the people trying to survive within them.

burden or best friend

SEARCH HISTORY

How to heal when someone ghosts you?

What is the psychology behind ghosting?

Can a friendship breakup be traumatic?

Why can't I block someone that has blocked
me on Instagram 2022?

"My best friend doesn't want to talk to me anymore" quotes

Is silent treatment the same as ghosting?

What are the stages of abandonment?
Are there stages?

Getting over someone that ghosted you

This is a snippet of my search history shortly after one of my best friends stopped speaking to me around the one-year mark of my dad's death. The frantic Google searches were an attempt to tame my crushing anxiety but they only made it worse.

My search history has always been a source of hilarity and anxiety, a window into my bustling brain and insatiable appetite for knowledge—and punishment. I was recently diagnosed with ADHD, so that checks out.

You can tell a lot about a person by their search history. If I die suddenly, more specifically if I cannot erase it in time, my synopsis might read:

"Angela had relational challenges she fought hard to understand, watched A LOT of cat videos and wasted loads of precious time on unpaid cult research."

On my dad's first anniversary of his death, I was so disheartened over our friendship potentially ending that I could barely move my limbs to get to the car to spend time outside.

I exhaled. My year of "firsts"—was over.

I sat on a rock and looked out at the ocean, feeling gutted by the assumption that her fleeing from my sad ass was a long time coming. I was a little preoccupied with other stuff, i.e. my dead dad and friend and dwindling health from the stress of the last year, to recognize I was slowly being broken up with and about to be ghosted.

As time passed, the grimness of her silence set in. That's when I coined a new term: *bitter grief.*

Bitter grief is when you refuse to deal with the added grief to grief that is already crushing your insides. You are so furious about it because you know eventually you will cry into a pillow and loudly play "Nothing Compares to You" by Sinead O'Connor while your partner tries not to stare.

"This can't be happening. This can't happen," was the mantra that took up mental and emotional space I didn't have. I dug my heels in for as long as I could, unwilling to grieve one more ounce, especially for someone who left my life in that fashion: no conversation, never an explanation. She was gone from my life, just like another death.

I struggled to comprehend how I could go from being a pending future bridesmaid to never speaking again? I'd even saved the cut of diamond she wanted in a photo album on my phone for when her boyfriend popped the question, damn it.

I'm not one to ogle at engagement rings or wedding dresses. I dislike being in weddings. I don't love random people looking at me, especially while wearing a dress and heels I can barely stand in. We can thank my first communion for that forever being a reality: never stepping foot in a white dress again. *Amen.*

I'm not too fond of games, so the stag and doe at a damp community center doesn't appeal to me. Neither do the "fun games" at bridal showers, and yet, for someone I love, my Italian roots kick into high gear: I make finger sandwiches or call the caterer, plan bachelorette parties, betray my every instinct to flee the scene due to not loving big gatherings, buy gifts, spend money I don't have and act like an emotional support animal armed with tissues for tears, lipstick for reapplication, and a bottle of Avion spray on a hot summer day.

I have been a Maid of Honour once and a bridesmaid twice. I did the things and would have done them again with vigour and pride because you do your best for your friends, even if wedding showers, baby showers, large group games and finger foods are not your thing. I naively assumed it also applied to not abandoning each other when you can barely breathe and are lost in grief.

Let me poorly paraphrase one of the articles that popped up from what looked like the search history of a thirteen year old girl, found on the number one trusted source for relationships (joking), the Cosmopolitan website.

"7 WAYS TO SURVIVE A BFF BREAKUP"

The best friend you vented about breakups to has now become the subject of the breakup, and it sucks bad.

Thanks for the reminder Dr. Bonior, author and adjunct professor of Psychology at Georgetown University, who shares the best ways to cope with this absolute shitstorm.

1. **Don't force closure.**

To that, I say, too late. I am the queen of leaving no stone unturned. I texted her a year later, hoping to repair the damage. We got together, and I ended up worse off than being ghosted. Note taken. Next:

2. **Tailor your social media if needed.**

She warns that this could look petty and aggressive to some, but my motto is all is fair in failed relationships. You don't need a painful reminder, especially if you're already grieving a profound loss.

And last, my absolute non-favourite:

3. **Accept that you may never speak to this person again.**

What every grief-stricken person wants to hear as they grieve a dead loved one is that your friendship is now dead too. That's a lot of dead to take in. No one grieving is trying to steal anyone's good vibes unless they are an asshole. There is such a thing as grieving assholes, but most of us are just trying to survive.

Was I overly sensitive in that first year? Yes. Was I the best friend I could have been while grieving two significant deaths? Nope, but there is a difference between being a shit friend across the board vs a temporary adjustment to life changing grief and gradually gaining back capacity to an equal relationship. Was my sad energy draining her? Probably. Was all this a deal breaker? Apparently, yes. It is also why I filled in many destructive blanks and why my therapist would have to pull me out each time.

When she stopped speaking to me, I plummeted into a downward spiral for longer than I would like to admit, not once, but twice! That's on me.

I felt deep shame that if one of my best friends could leave me in this way, my grief must be too much. "I was too much," even for some people I called best friends. It wasn't true, but it felt that way at the time. Not everyone can stick around for the death stuff, but it doesn't mean it didn't rip me into pieces. See, *Bitter Grief.*

Relationship ruptures are inevitable in grief unless your entire friend group and family are a posse of well-adjusted unicorns with no trauma or childhood wounds.

People's capacity for gut-wrenching circumstances does not miraculously expand because you need it to, and neither does yours. People don't morph into qualified therapists. I wish that's how it worked. People's experiences, reactions to big emotions, (especially not their own) trauma responses, communication style, attachment wounds, and the like don't disappear because you're grieving, and neither do yours.

They become amplified.

Anger is felt, sadness surfaces, and despair may be present for a time but like the grief I was already grappling with, the sharp edges dulled.

Grief can change relationships, highlight the ways they were not working, and bring forth gratitude for those who can continue to be by our side. Plenty of people extended grace to me as I dealt with these life-changing losses. The *good-ish* news, the part I can control is to continue expanding my capacity and ability to cope with my grief (I do) and heal the trauma that I experienced from these losses (I am).

DEAR FRIENDS WHO STUCK AROUND,

If I have told you, "let's connect," and we haven't, or we set up a time to chat and I didn't follow through, I am sorry. I am grieving, not working at full capacity. Some days I feel back to my old self, but then I remember that I am no longer that person.

When I make plans and break them, I retreat into my grief shell. This must be confusing for you. I seem reliable and connected, then I am gone. It is hard to explain what is happening day to day.

You see, grieving is learning a whole new way of being in my body, heart, and brain.

Patience is hard enough for me: patience from you means everything to me as I navigate this new terrain.

Please don't forget me as I grieve. Please check in with me. Please be patient and show up for me; losing ____________ is the hardest thing I have ever faced.

Love,

(Your name here)

Where there is immense love, there is profound grief.

LOVE NOTES 4

relationship grief

Allow yourself to grieve when a friendship ends.

Secondary loss is all too common when grieving the death of a loved one.

We tend to dismiss this kind of grief. If this person meant a lot to you, don't bypass the pain. Endings hurt.

Let yourself feel it.

Let it burn.

People may try to minimize your grief to make themselves feel more comfortable with it.

That isn't about you.

Their response is a window into what they can or can't tolerate.

Death is bringing up a discomfort in them. It is ok to create space and boundaries with people like this if they are causing you more pain.

I have learned that if there was already a strain on a relationship, it is revealed even more so when you are grieving.

You do not just grieve the person who has died. You mourn all the people who can't fully show up for the hard stuff.

In grief, you get the stripped-down version of yourself.

It is hard to fake anything when you are grieving a significant loss.

It offers raw, unfiltered truths.

Some will stick around and love you through it.

Some will run the other way.

The raw response to grief is beyond other peoples' understanding if they have not lived it yet. It puts "your loved one may die, too" on a billboard sign.

You may wake up one morning without them.

Even if we logically know this, facing it head-on is entirely different.

The antidote is to tune into our body's response and not project our discomfort back onto them. To listen to what our bodies are saying.

To respect our limits, tend to our nervous systems and return to connection when ready.

It is a practice to be with the feelings that are coming up and not push it away. It asks us to slow down and be with ourselves so we can be with each other.

You are grieving, and that automatically puts your relationships under a microscope.

It is a chance for friends to offer unwavering support or show you they have no space for it.

The fickleness of relationships is felt.

A deep reverence for friends who can be there through your hardest moments emerges.

Your darkest times become something that brings you closer together, not further apart.

How people—not all, but some—respond to your pain may end the relationship, and it will be people you care for immensely.

The relationship as you knew it changed shape and morphed into something you no longer recognize.

Grief does that. Secondary loss feels cruel—one part lousy timing and two parts heartbreaking.

Some responses to your pain won't feel supportive or kind. Keep showing up for yourself. Build relationships with people who see you. Build capacity for yourself.

In grief, our wounds come up against other people's wounds. Grief isn't the equalizer we think it is. Healthy relationships are built on trust, hearing one another, empathy, understanding, safety and self-awareness. It is something to work towards together. We must expand our capacity so we don't leave when things get hard but hold steady and love each other back to life.

You are grieving, and grieving is
all-consuming. It is ok to grieve fully, even if it
is hard to explain to others.

Grief will have you questioning some of your
relationships.

When people in your life have not
experienced this kind of pain or deal with it
differently, it can make for complex dynamics,
conflict, and communication breakdowns.

Find respite talking to people and other
grievers who respect where you are at, the
ones that understand this kind of brokenness
and love you through it.

DEAD DAD CARD — PART ONE

Here is a cringe-worthy example of how brain-fogged, boundaryless, and raw grief can manifest in the early days and months after the death of a loved one.

I have clocked enough therapy hours in the last few years to know there is no shame in stumbling through painful life events. It's called *survival.*

I take responsibility for my relational mishaps, as they connect to grief. I laughed at myself, as did my partner and close friends, when my default setting in acute grief was acting as if I were on my deathbed.

I felt an urgency to right certain wrongs in my life—a puddle of pain, I looked for comfort and closure in all the wrong places. My naive motto? We are all going to die at any moment; it could be your turn next, or mine. Let's sing kumbaya and be decent humans to each other.

I brought a casserole to a sword fight.

I watched my dad work through his unfinished business at the end of his life, acting as his connection point to others. He would bring up someone he hadn't seen in ages, even some I didn't know. "Do you want me to try to get a hold of them?" I would ask. I could tell he was struggling with events and relationships from his past, while he also shared with me fond memories in his makeshift hospital bed in the dining room.

For the most part, I knew the reasons why he didn't want to connect with some of the people he mentioned, a falling out that never got repaired, but I could sense the sorrow in his voice. Even with his death looming, there were people he did not want to see. The ship had sailed.

My compulsion to address my own unresolved conflicts, and to reconnect with people from my past felt like a peculiar response because I was not the one dying. I was alive, but maybe it was because cumulative grief felt like death. Perhaps that's why his experience rubbed off on me. I, too, felt the urge to partake in a preemptive life review. *When in Rome.*

My manner of mourning had become burdened by a temporary amnesia of the fallout between myself and others, and the reasons there was a distance placed between us.

My lamenting brain thought, "Hey girl, why not rustle up some skeletons in your closet to spice things up while you go through the worst pain of your life?"

I was hopeful that one of my exes would acknowledge the death stuff. I was on satisfactory terms with nearly all of them once we both moved on.

I emailed to tell him my dad had died. I should have taken the hint when he wanted nothing to do with me as we mourned our mutual friend, T, who died by suicide a few months earlier. So why would my dad be any different?

I remained hopeful for an empathetic response and for him to recognize the gravity of this loss for my family and others who were closely connected to him for many years, including him. This exercise would soon showcase its own substantial lapse in judgment.

When I got his reply, my whole body went numb as I stared at my phone.

My since deleted email was likely a string of nonsensical sentences I would pay good money to take back if I could. I don't recall much of what I said, but if there was a time I needed some grace for the state I was in, this was it. His words felt like vengeance, the timing cruel, but the overtone of his email was loud and clear: "leave me alone." I respected his boundary but neither his timing nor delivery.

My grief-stricken thought was that someone who had spent an intimate amount of time with my family and me, someone who had held my grandmother's hand, someone who shared linens, someone who knew my parents more than most, the thought that this someone might not want to know that my dad had died—this thought was unfathomable. Avoidance is bliss, perhaps? Or he disliked me more than I had realized.

I guess I'll never know.

DEAD DAD CARD — PART TWO

> "Grief is a heart-wrenchingly painful problem for the brain to solve, and grieving necessitates learning to live in the world with the absence of someone you love deeply, who is ingrained in your understanding of the world. This means that for the brain, your loved one is simultaneously gone and also everlasting."
>
> —*Mary-Frances O'Connor*

As I mourned in the early days, I resorted to magical thinking that some of my past relationships or even some of my present ones were healthier than they are. It was a hard crash when I realized that my fictional deathbed pipe dream of healing past hurts would not be happening. I felt mortified for making contact with certain people from my past while in a grief vortex once I came out of the fog.

Magical thinking can also look like hoping your dead someone will walk through the door or thinking you saw them on the street corner. Trying to locate your loved one that has died when you're in shock or in the early days/months is common. It takes time to adjust to never seeing them again.

Some nights after work, I called my dad to tell him about my day. It was a blow to my heart whenever I searched for my phone to call him in my early grief days. "Your dad," a voice would softly say, "is dead."

It takes capacity for your brain to remember something has changed. While no, they may not be walking through the door, or answering their cell, or asking about your day, your attachment to your loved one who has died has not and will not change.

Missing his physical presence, I looked for ways to feel close to him, to help me cope with the drastic changes in my new life-altering environment.

For weeks, I slept in my dad's sweater that he wore when he was sick, with my friend's scarf draped around my neck, trying to feel closer to them. At the time, it brought me comfort. I looked foolish, but didn't care.

I am playing the dead dad card because I refuse to go down another shame spiral for this gross miscalculation of what I thought was death etiquette. I need acknowledgement. In my defence, a friend's mother died around the same time as my dad, and her ex flew from the United States to Canada for the funeral. Her ex got on a damn plane, and mine couldn't muster the words "So sorry for your loss." What was wrong with people? I cried when she told me this.

That conversation confirmed that I wasn't delusional but making questionable decisions about who to trust with my immense grief.

A year later, my high school boyfriend sent me a Facebook message:

> "I've been wanting to say I'm really sorry to hear about your dad. I read some article a while ago you wrote and thought it was great, and I really wanted to give you my condolences."

I made similarly poor judgments that led to me saying yes to someone coming to my dad's funeral from my past who should have stayed there. I thought it was a kind gesture, but two days later, drama ensued.

I do not recommend adding to your grief pile by expecting people to be different than they are because your loved one died. Grief invited some of my past traumas to resurface, and I tended to these past hurts with a therapist. This is ongoing; I am a work-in-progress.

Becoming the messiest version of myself has allowed me to see what wasn't working in my relationships, past and present, and to start to move forward in my life. I needed to learn what personal responsibility was. I needed to stop forcing a happier ending to relationships already dead and buried. These were not my people anymore, but my grief brain didn't know the difference.

I saw the death of someone as a time to put differences aside, let bygones be bygones and or pay respect to what was. That doesn't mean that others think that way too. Maybe I have watched too many unrealistic movies but now I can look at it for what it was:

a reflex

a trauma response and a human
reaction to loss and not wanting more
pain, past or present—

a desire to relate, love, and heal past
wounds with people I still cared for—

a deathbed reaction without a death.

LOVE NOTES 5

boundaries in grief

In grief, your boundaries are sacred.

In grief, your body needs rest.

In grief, your nervous system needs tending.

In grief, you need to do what is necessary to protect what little energy you have.

In grief, you need understanding.

We are blessed to be gifted **grace**. I hope you know
the feeling when someone shows you it
is possible.

Self-betrayal can look like staying in
relationships that no longer feel like home.

SHOW UP FOR THE GRIEVING

If people in your life haven't experienced the death of someone they love or whatever loss you are facing, divorce, a friend break up, a health crisis, infertility, a life-changing injury, mental health struggle, job loss, or climate disaster, they may be unsure how to support you.

Even if they have, they may project how they handled their grief and expect the same from you.

Given that many people are grappling with the dominant culture's spell to be preoccupied, numbed out and weighed down by busyness, most people are already overwhelmed with their life issues, obligations, individual goals, and dreams. It can be challenging for some people to show up in meaningful ways for others.

This lack of capacity to show up, mixed with the exhaustion from your grief, can cause misunderstandings, frustration and anger, leading to a rupture that goes unrepaired, potentially ruining the connection.

Whether tangible or emotional support, it feels good to know people are there for you beyond the first few weeks and months. I call those days the vortex. Time becomes nothing at all. You're simply trying to survive, and if people around you are making that time more challenging than it already is, there will be upheaval.

Not everyone can be there for you, which becomes apparent in these heartbreaking instances, but grief support can look like this.

EARLY GRIEF: EXAMPLES OF SUPPORT

Kindly gives you space if you ask for it.

Showing up at the funeral or, if unable to make it, offering support in another way with an effort that says, "I see you, and I want to be here for you." And actually be there.

Ask to drop food off at your door.
Sharing a meal when you feel up to it.
Going for a walk together.
Sending a care package.
Checking in via text or phone call, without expecting a quick reply.
Not checking in as much if it's too overwhelming. A simple, "I'm here."

ONGOING SUPPORT

Being there for the big stuff, a birthday, death date, in person, a text, or a phone call if that is important.

Them asking you what you need from them.

Be a good ear by listening to what you are going through.

None of these things will make grief disappear, but it is a gesture that suggests,

"I care about you. I want you to know I'm here and thinking of you. I want to be in a relationship with you, even as you are grieving, even when it gets hard, even when you are lost, confused and sensitive."

Adjust your expectations to the different levels of the relationships you find yourself in. While it is heartbreaking, some may find it too much to support you.

They may state things like, "you need to move on," instead of kindly addressing concern for your well-being. They may become frustrated with you. If they react this way, it could be their unprocessed grief, trauma, or past wounds surfacing. They could feel triggered by the sudden change in you and thus become unsure of how to respond.

There are many reasons people melt down in the face of someone else's grief. Try not to take it personally, especially if they aren't explaining themselves.

If you express that you feel unsupported, they may have a stress response; they might kick it into people-pleasing mode, or become resentful, defensive, combative or do nothing at all. *Fight, flight, freeze, fawn.*

For many, in the early days and months of grief, it's hard to navigate relational strains. If you can be honest with the person making things harder on you, take the space to gather yourself and continue to meet your own needs.

This can be frustrating to someone in acute grief. Two people are attempting to relate to life-altering circumstances, and it is challenging to think of someone else's feelings first, right?

It can be difficult to see outside your grief when you are in the throes of it.

Some people will surprise you. They may eventually own how they weren't there for you or admit that they caused more stress or harm. I respect people like this. It takes courage to own our mistakes, which goes both ways.

It is a vulnerable act to make an effort to build trust after a rupture takes place. Grief can heighten your relational wounds. It can also cause overreactions. You may become self-protective around people that have the potential to cause more pain. They are not attached in the same way to the person that has died, and now something as big as grief is challenging the relational bond you have (or had). The magnitude of your distress has you fumbling around, and the same goes for people who love you.

ACUTE GRIEF RESPONSE

> "Grief is subversive, undermining the quiet agreement to behave and be in control of our emotions. It is an act of protest that declares our refusal to live numb and small. There is something feral about grief, something essentially outside the ordained and sanctioned behaviors of our culture."
>
> —*Francis Weller*

When I got the text message from my friend's mom telling me that her daughter had taken her life, I gripped my stomach and bent my chest over my knees. Nauseous and lightheaded, my body went into a protective position. I called to ensure I hadn't misread her text. I wept when she told me again.

Receiving that kind of news over the phone or via text message is as bad as you might already know.

I canceled my massage patients for the day and began calling some of her friends on the mother's behalf. I started each call saying, "Where are you?" "Are you driving?" "Are you able to sit down?"

Throughout the day, my throat slowly became constricted. I frequently coughed and cleared my throat, attempting to get more air into my lungs. A consistent pounding headache from crying would soon make a home in the base of my skull and behind my right eye for years to come.

The acute stress response to a significant loss can be alarming for those experiencing and witnessing it. I have seen enough movies that touch on acute grief to know what it looks and sounds like, yet I was not prepared for how it would feel in my body.

Everyone responds differently to shocking news. A sudden loss, like my friend's death, can have a range of responses. Some people wail and fall to their knees, curl up into a ball, or thrash and scream, and yet others grow silent and still. Some sob uncontrollably but wait until they are alone, some show no emotion at all, and others shut down, quietly retreating inward.

We are quick to judge how we think people *should* act in the face of a tragic loss or death but there is not one way. There is only your way.

LOVE NOTES 6

grief, your way

Let your heart break. Love is still waiting for you to come home.

Be broken, alive, and free from the pressures to be someone else's definition of whole.

Grieving can feel like a tsunami—a body that floods with every emotion you have ever felt that comes to you all at once, without preparation.

It may be uncomfortable to describe what you are feeling, and some people may not understand, but that doesn't make you difficult to love. It makes you human, and being a grieving human is hard.

LOVE NOTES 7

affirmations

We live in a society that enables you to bypass your pain and clutch at the denial of death until it's on your front doorstep. Although it is a common thread amongst us, it is still a disservice—to be sheltered from the inevitable. We are ill-equipped from our death-avoidant upbringings, reliant on our parents' failed teachings on approaches to death and grieving. It echoes the cultural messaging to create distance from it—encouraging social acceptance over being in a relationship with one's grief.

Saying the word *died* is too much for some people. To soften it, we use the socially accepted euphemisms *passed away* or *we lost them.* I'm not too fond of these sayings, even if I sometimes use them for ease and acceptance. If you prefer it over *dead, died, die,* I understand.

That is why we have these substitutions in the first place, to soften death's sharp edges and not scare people off. The grief rebel in me wants to call it what it is—that someone we love *died.* They did not get lost in the woods, did not wander off, did not fly away in the night. They died... and as a result, what we have lost because of their death bears an agonizing list of things that have unceremoniously changed our entire worlds.

Dominant culture commends people for getting things done in a timely manner—grief changes that notion. The people in your life want you to be ok, but we don't hold enough space for "becoming ok." Depending on the loss, this takes more time than one might think.

Say this with me:

I am here.

I am whole, and this is hard.

My grief deserves space.

My heart is broken and mending.

I tend to my grief and honour my love.

Continue to make space for yourself
to grieve.

Be honest about your pain to those
who love you.

I know how hard you try to be strong
for others.

Grief is tended to.
There is no finish line.

The depth of our feelings is a gift, but we live in a society that wants us busy, distracted and disconnected from this depth.

The healing is in the grief **rituals**.

The healing is letting yourself **ache**.

The healing is in the **community** you keep.

The healing is in **love**.

The healing is in **self-awareness**.

The healing is in **taking responsibility**.

The healing is **knowing** the broken parts of our society and not falling for them.

Tragedies don't

"happen for a reason."

Tragedies happen,

and it changes someone's

entire world.

WHEN IN THE DEPTHS

> "It is so important to have ways to release those pains to keep clearing ourselves. Hanging on to old pain just makes it grow until it smothers our creativity, our joy, and our ability to connect with others. It may even kill us. Often my community uses grief rituals to heal wounds and open us to spirit's call."
>
> —*Sobonfu Somé*

People's lack of grief-literacy is one of the many reasons you must remember your power in times of grief. You won't always have the ideal support and understanding from those around you.

I have connected with fellow grievers who share their painful stories with me through social media. They confess they felt utterly alone once the funeral was over or well before it.

Witnessing me in the depth of my non-silver-lining grief vortex was too much for some people, but grief is relational. We need each other as we grieve; yet not having someone to lean on as time passes is a regular occurrence.

Dysfunctional family dynamics, friendships going awry, lack of relational skills, grief illiteracy from yourself and others, trauma, underlying mental health issues, not receiving professional support when it's needed, workplace pressures and strained communication in marriage or partnership–any or all of these can result in the griever feeling alone—isolated.

You need support from the people in your life in the depths of grief, but our experiences aren't one-size-fits-all, which means the way people want to be supported will look different. Multiple people grieving the same person adds to the complexity.

People can become strangers in grief. Your best friend can become a stranger. Your partner can become a stranger. Sometimes you don't realize it until you go through a life-changing experience. People may freeze up around you due to their nervous systems' response to your grief. Death can create a stress response in those close to you: family, friends, acquaintances, colleagues, and even strangers can become uncomfortable in your presence. Most people are not trying to make you feel worse than you already do. However, their discomfort may have them react instead of respond, which can result in them saying something insensitive, or being unsupportive.

Later on, it can be hard to extend yourself to people who disappointed you. The focus is on keeping your head above water. It feels impossible to take on another hard thing, a hard conversation, a defensive reaction instead of compassion becomes too much for you to bear. There are certain relationships you will let go of. Some people will rub you the wrong way. Some of those relationships will be mended, but some may not.

As you expand around your grief, it still may be hard to extend yourself to people who disappointed you. It is such a vulnerable act to reach out and when you realize how much you have changed and how little they understood what you went through. Many won't ask.

Do you feel like people are being difficult or unsupportive? Sometimes it's true, but most of the time, it's not.

They, too, are responding to your loss, the sad you, the angry you, the unreasonable you, the "griefy" you. Their lack of understanding of what you're going through or went through magnifies what you're already feeling.

This doesn't mean that abuse of any kind is ok, it's never ok, but healthy relating mostly comes down to skills, capacity, effort and a boatload of grace.

WHEN PANDEMIC STRIKES

On March 11th, 2020, the World Health Organization declared COVID-19 a global pandemic. As I counted the days to my dad's death anniversary on March 15th, I watched the world come undone. Looking back on the agonizing year I had gone through, I braced for what was to come collectively.

Witnessing a loved one die or, in my case, three loved ones in a short time—my beloved grandmother died during peak covid in April 2020—was excruciating.

We endured the shared heartbreak of a global pandemic resulting in mass deaths, postponed funerals, drawn-out separation from loved ones, and gut-wrenching last goodbyes via FaceTime or phone call. With that also came a subset of people's responses to the pandemic with fear-fueled repudiation that the pandemic was a hoax and shaming people's health status as a moral failing if they presented with comorbidities. This collective fear response sent me down a different kind of sorrowful spiral.

I felt a fierce protective instinct as loved ones' deaths were reduced to statistics or used as talking points, diminishing the gravity of having a loved one die of COVID-19.

During therapy sessions, I sat sobbing with deep sadness as I pondered all those whose loved ones died in isolation. Some of that therapy time was spent trying to make sense of what was happening globally.

These responses illuminated the North American dominant culture's inability to withstand the discomfort around uncertainty and death.

LOVE NOTES 8

after notes

It just takes

one loving person

to believe that

your story matters.

Because it does.

It feels good to be with people

who don't need you to pretend.

In grief, time takes on new meaning.

Death dates and countdowns are now measured and felt differently.

One half enjoys who is still with you, and the other misses who you grieve.

It is hard to get through all the firsts, seconds, and beyond.

Time feels different because you are.

No matter how long ago your loved one died,
your grief matters.

Your grief deserves a voice.

You deserve space to feel the love for your
person and honour them in whatever way
feels good to you.

In a society that encourages people to pretend, your grief is a rebellious act.

In grief, we are sometimes forced to pretend.
You don't have to.

You are allowed to figure out what hurts and
let it have space.

Your pain is valid, even when it's too much,
even when it seems irrational and messy, even
when it's hard to explain, and even when
people walk away.

It feels complicated and complex because it is.

Grief is uprooting and disorientating, yet we
find our way through the pain.

Rituals make all the difference, like nightly candle lighting or wearing our loved one's clothing.

Not knowing

how to show up

but doing it anyway

is the act of love

and connection

we are all hungry for.

Please remember not to force yourself to
search for the "gifts in your grief."

There is so much pressure on grievers to do
this right away. People pushing you to "see the good"
or the silver linings feels awful when
you are in the depths of your grief.

It is not their place to speak to something you
must seek on your own. Do not let anyone
force this on you, not until you are ready to
accept that for yourself.

I was in so much pain that when people tried
to offer up the gifts that grief brings, I silently
raged.

Your grief can bring you to places that you were scared to go before.

You may need professional support.

There is no shame in healing trauma that is awakened by your grief.

Your healing is your legacy.

Choose wisely with whom you

share your heart.

Share your grief if that feels good. Break the taboo.

Ask for something different. Ask for people to become grief literate.

Call for vulnerability and a deeper understanding.

It is possible to shift the culture into being more empathetic and connected to ourselves and each other.

In grieving authentically for yourself, you're gifting others freedom to grieve more truly.

Your grief matters.

You are the only one who understands the depth of the pain you feel, for it is yours and yours alone.

People do their best to empathize, but they do not inherit the shattering in your bones.

You hope for patience and understanding from those around you, praying that your grief will not be invalidated, diminished, minimized because if there were one true betrayal, it would be this.

You withdraw into your proverbial cave, come out and then go back again when you need to tend to your grief.

There is before the death of your loved one and after. There is before the breaking and after. And that is all.

EYE LINES

You often find the death and grieving section at bookstores on a bottom shelf. I find that to be another sign of our death-phobic society—our stories hidden away, unpopular comparatively to other genres, our pain left to languish, even though death and grief impact every one of us.

I hope the dying and grieving section expands and reaches people's eye lines on bookshelves. To find comfort in the pages of grief writing when you inevitably find yourself with the wind knocked out of you, well beyond your limit of what you can handle but have no choice but to face the reality of a loved one's death or life-changing situation.

Grief gatherings, grief education, philosophers, elders, death workers, death doulas, herbalists, celebrants, grief therapists, somatic practitioners, non-cultish spiritual leaders, chaplains, solid friends and partners—each one can walk alongside you, supporting, not hindering the natural course of grieving, which is to learn to be with it.

In my life, rituals bridged the gap from "this is too painful" to feeling comforted by forming a new way to connect and honour my dad, friend and grandmother. A ritual is anything done with intention and care. This kept me afloat in times of deep sorrow; candle lighting in the evenings and creating an altar with my loved ones' belongings and pictures placed in the part of the house where I could see them. The beach walk my partner and

I take every death anniversary for my dad, the ring I wear with my dad's ashes in it, always worn so he can come with me on adventures. The daily showers also counted as a ritual when I could barely get off Couch Island. In the early grief days, everything in my life became infused with ritual. Everything felt like a sacred act. Every inch of me needed to savour and preserve the feeling of having loved someone so profoundly, losing them and now finding ways to still be with them. This has become a beautiful part of me.

The external noise and dominant culture's encouragement to disconnect from self and societal pressures to conform pull you out of your experience. Urging you to perform a quick and even a false "recovery" that usually results in hiding away pain.

Your body knows how to respond to loss. It's a biological reflex to grieve your attachment to someone now gone. The attachment never severs, so why pretend it does?

You never stop loving those who have died yet honour that there are exceptions: for instance, you might feel relieved once a loved one has died, if the relationship was shaky.

Grief looks and feels different because we are different from one another, and so are our relationships.

I often think about those I have loved and am no longer connected with. I shared about some of those people in this book. For them, I carry a different kind of ache which I feel in my quieter moments. I remind myself to let go of the stories I felt entitled to, which only keep me in more pain. It just is. Relationships shift and change. We are all learning and trying to cope in different ways.

In grief, we have the opportunity to learn to be with what is and to focus on nourishing the relationships of mutual respect, effort, love, grace, support and kindness. That can be a beautiful way forward. This is where I live now.

I laugh at my perceived notion of how I thought people *should* act toward me and my grief. While you're in the depths of it, it's difficult to relate. The focus is on trying to understand our private suffering. To survive it. When there is too much pain to hold, it's hard to see outside yourself, which I learned slowly and with time. People are living their unshattered lives and I am still piecing mine back together.

When people gather for the grieving, to breathe life back into them as they weep, to hold their tired bodies so they can rest and then rise—unhurriedly, allowing sadness to lead. However long it takes, bit by bit. Life starts to gain colour again.

No one is asking anyone to take on their grief as their own. You never ask someone to fix it because you know it can't be. You make grief a home. You learn the grief dance.

No one can prepare you for your response to the death of a loved one. You can look to those that have faced death before you or whose cultures did not get severed from their rituals, the inner knowledge around death and grief, and how vital communal support is in grief.

You have a chance to reclaim what is rightfully yours, a connection to your loved one that is no longer here, and a connection to your ancestors' ways of living with grief and grieving before it got watered down to stages and pathology.

You can't bury grief. It asks you to soften and to listen. It only gets louder until you do.

ACKNOWLEDGEMENTS

Thank you, Mo Duffy Cobb and Genevieve Loughlin, my publishers, for bringing this book into being and believing in my writing and work. Thank you as well to my editors Danielle and Mo.

Thank you to my family and extended family and my partner's family, especially my mom. She is the lighthouse in the dark storm, my anchor in grief, my first phone call when I need a chat, and who shares my writing with her friends and believes in me even when I don't.

My dear friends, some I will name here that helped me through some of my darkest days, showed me grace and brought me back to life. Some that were also early readers, Leslie, Willow, and Shauna also for her grief and trauma education, Ariel, Jen, David, Mandi, Kaley, Jord, Lindsay, Ashleigh, Sheena, Rachel, Pat, Ed, Shannon, Litsa and my two therapists, sometimes you've got to pull in the major leaguers.

I also want to thank those who read and shared my writings on grief and loss these past three years and for making it more than just some ramblings on social media.

Research states that animals far outperform the grief support of nurses and friends: https://www.madinamerica.com/2021/06/pets-effective-grief-support-humans-study-finds/

With that in mind, I will also thank my precious cat, Cheddar, who showed up on our doorstep shortly after my dad died. Disclaimer: We brought her back to her owners down the street, and she kept coming back, and they were ok with it. She chose us. She decided to stay with my grieving ass, and it's what I needed, someone to show up in this way and love me as I was, in grief. I didn't think it would be in the form of a tabby cat with half of a tail. The joyful distraction from heartbreak was a welcomed respite.

I would also like to thank pizza for boosting me with tryptophan. The psychologist that diagnosed me with ADHD, (finally things make a little more sense) and audiobooks that kept me company when I couldn't sleep.

Last and most important, my partner, Ciaran, thank you for loving me, holding me up, not judging me, for letting me grieve my way, and for reading these pages out loud to me not once but twice. Thanks for believing in me, and showing me what unconditional love and healthy attachment from a partner is. Thank you for gently letting me know that the time I cried about the "Christmas cookies" was not about the cookies but my dead dad. I love you—a true talent to be able to make me laugh even when I was incredibly sad.

WEBSITES

* *Shauna Janz Grief and Resiliency, Education, Facilitation and Mentorship* | shaunajanz.com
* *What's Your Grief* | whatsyourgrief.com
* *The Grief Well Village* | www.thegriefwell.ca
* *Alica Forneret* | alicaforneret.com
* *Modern Loss* | modernloss.com
* *Help Texts* | helptexts.com

GRIEF BOOKS

* *The Grieving Brain: The Surprising Science of How We Learn from Love and Loss* by Mary-Frances O'Connor (Harper One, 2022)
* *The Year of Magical Thinking* by Joan Didion (Vintage International, 2007)
* *The Wild Edge of Sorrow: Rituals of Renewal and the Sacred Work of Grief* by Francis Weller (North Atlantic Books, 2015)
* *Bearing the Unbearable: Love, Loss, and the Heartbreaking Path of Grief* by Joanne Cacciatore (Wisdom Publication, 2017)
* *What's Your Grief? Lists to Help You Through Any Loss* by Eleanor Haley MS, Litsa Williams MA LCSW-C (Quirk Books, 2022)
* *Anxiety: The Missing Stage of Grief, A Revolutionary Approach to Understanding and Healing the Impact of Los*s by Claire Bidwell Smith (Da Capo Lifelong Books, 2018)
* *The Baby Loss Guide* by Zoë Clark-Coates (2021)
* *It's OK That You're Not OK: Meeting Grief and Loss in a Culture That Doesn't Understand* by Megan Devine (Sounds True, 2017)

RESEARCH

* Stroebe, M., Schut, H., & Finkenauer, C. (2001). The traumatization of grief? A conceptual framework for understanding the trauma-bereavement interface. *The Israel journal of psychiatry and related sciences*, 38(3-4), 185–201.
* Harris D. (2009). Oppression of the bereaved: a critical analysis of grief in Western society. *Omega, 60(3)*, 241–253.
* Sillis, L., Claes, L., Andreissen, K.. (2022). Association between Grief and Somatic Complaints in Bereaved University and College Students. *International. Journal of Environmental Research and Public Health.*

ABOUT THE AUTHOR

After the death of her father, friend and grandmother in quick succession, Angela needed a channel to grieve these profound losses. Writing has always been her lifeline through hard times and grief from the loss of her loved ones was no different. Seeing how this helped her, Angela began to help others with their grief through her reflective writing on her social media channels.

She offers people a soft space to land as they navigate their grief without judgement. Angela provides reflective writing for grievers who have lost something or someone dear to them. They walk together differently through their healing journey of learning to grow with their grief, not move on from it.